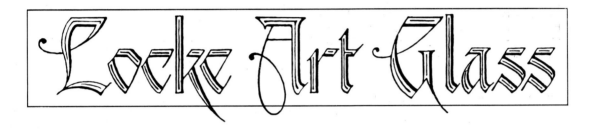

A Guide for Collectors

With Photographic Illustrations

of 190 Examples

by JOSEPH H. *and* JANE T. LOCKE

Dover Publications, Inc.
New York

Foreword

The art glass made by Joseph Locke has been sought by eager collectors for the past 30 years and has been well documented in many publications. Collectors who also found etched glasses labeled "Locke Art" or "Jo Locke" have long puzzled how to date and identify the patterns of the pieces. Until now, there has been almost no information available to collectors or museum curators about Locke's own glass-etching business, which he operated for many years.

At last Joseph H. Locke, grandson of the artist, has filled this gap by facilitating publication of the only known sales catalog of Locke Art Glassware. This catalog, dating from ca. 1905, was carried by the Locke Art salesman as he visited jewelry, china and department stores in the Northeast and Midwest. Following the usual practice with such catalogs, it consisted of photographs on loose-leaf pages so that pages could be added or deleted as the product line changed. Thus earlier but short-lived Locke designs, or those which are later, are not included here.

Mr. Locke has presented this catalog and other original Locke material to the library of The Corning Museum of Glass to make them available to all glass researchers. His generous gift is most appreciated. Collectors and curators everywhere will find this publication of great help in identifying Locke's glass.

Jane Shadel Spillman
Curator of American Glass
The Corning Museum of Glass

Copyright © 1987 by Joseph H. and Jane T. Locke.
Foreword copyright © 1987 by The Corning Museum of Glass.
All rights reserved under Pan American and International
Copyright Conventions.

Published in Canada by General Publishing Company, Ltd.,
30 Lesmill Road, Don Mills, Toronto, Ontario.
Published in the United Kingdom by Constable and Company, Ltd.,
10 Orange Street, London WC2H 7EG.

*Locke Art Glass: A Guide for Collectors / With
Photographic Illustrations of 190 Examples* is a new work, first published
by Dover Publications, Inc., in 1987.

Manufactured in the United States of America
Dover Publications, Inc.
31 East 2nd Street
Mineola, N.Y. 11501

Library of Congress Cataloging-in-Publication Data

Locke, Joseph H.
Locke art glass.

Bibliography: p.
1. Locke, Joseph, 1846–1936—Catalogs. 2. Glassware—
United States—History—19th century—Collectors and
collecting—Catalogs. 3. Glassware—United States—
History—20th century—Collectors and collecting—
Catalogs. I. Locke, Jane T. II. Title.
NK5198.L63A4 1987   748.2913   87-13416
ISBN 0-486-25400-3 (pbk.)

Preface

ANNUAL MEETING OF GLASS MEN, ATLANTIC CITY
July 20, 1905
The Locke Art Glassware Company of Mt. Oliver, Pennsylvania, has evolved a process by which the most delicate designs are reproduced . . . beautiful masterpieces in glassware . . . each individual piece a work of art equaling, if not surpassing, the best results of Bohemian and French glassmakers.
The Crockery and Glass Journal
July 20, 1905, p. 26

This book is an edited reproduction of the photographs from a sales catalog prepared by Joseph Locke at about the time these compliments were printed. The Locke Art Glassware salesman carried the original catalog as he visited china and jewelry shops across Pennsylvania, Ohio, New York, West Virginia, Maryland, Indiana, Michigan and Illinois, and in the District of Columbia.

The catalog consisted of 67 high-quality black-and-white photographs fastened into a standard leather-bound photograph album. It was a one-of-a-kind sales tool used in direct contact with the customer and/or the store representative. The salesman also carried supplies of sample glassware; on request, samples would be mailed to a store.

References are made throughout this book to a Locke Art Glassware sales-order book. This is a standard salesman's order book in which the sales were written up in longhand. It consists of the carbon copies, on tissue paper, of sales made by the salesman between October 3, 1906 and March 6, 1907. Information about sales statistics and wholesale prices and the names of the etched designs are taken from this original sales record.

Much of the information given here about the product line of Locke Art Glassware, and the nature of the decoration process, is based upon a personal survey made by Joseph H. and Jane T. Locke in 1985–86. Contact was made with other Locke grandchildren, and 11 major collections were studied, including museum, family and other private collections. This research has made it possible to relate the information in the catalog and the sales book to actual collection pieces.

The pictures of Locke Art Glassware shown here were taken by Joseph H. Locke for the original sales catalog. Many of the original photographs show considerable deterioration from age and exposure to light. Some of these pictures have been included here only because they indicate the shape of etched pieces that are not otherwise shown.

All photographs of the originals were processed and printed by Robert Arnold, great-grandson of Joseph Locke. Mr. Arnold has obtained the greatest possible degree of clarity in the images.

Information on prices and the names of the glass pieces are taken from the original catalog. However, the names of the etched decorations, not included in the catalog, are taken from the sales-order book or have been created by the authors.

We recognize that there are glassware shapes and etched designs in collections of Locke Art Glassware that are not shown in this book. These pieces predate the catalog or were introduced at a later time. Research will be necessary to document and photograph these additional pieces for later publication.

Joseph H. Locke
Lantana, Florida
1987

Acknowledgments

We want to thank the following people for their contributions to the conception and development of this book. They are listed in the general chronological order of the assistance given.

Michael Malley, a Pittsburgh antique dealer, insisted that we do something with the Joseph Locke artifacts before it was too late. Rege and Mary Ferson, who recently published their own book, while warning us of all the pitfalls and effort entailed in authorship, also encouraged us. Doctor Michael T. Stieber, Archivist and Senior Research Scientist at the Hunt Institute for Botanical Documentation, Carnegie-Mellon University, and Lindsay Bond Totten, Botanist and Director of the Pittsburgh Garden Center, identified a number of the flowers and shrubs depicted in the Locke Art Glass catalog. John G. Labanish and William F. Trimble of the Historical Society of Western Pennsylvania helped us streamline the project into achievable form. Eunice Evans, granddaughter of Joseph Locke who lived with him as an adult, gave excellent family advice. Kenneth Locke, grandson of Joseph Locke, and his wife Phyllis provided family perspective and assistance throughout the process. Ann Weiss, of the University of Pittsburgh Department of Fine Arts, researched the "antiquity" patterns and discovered the goddess Nut in the Egyptian design. Miriam Mucha, while President of the National Early American Glass Club, gave the manuscript a timely reading, and offered excellent criticism and advice regarding the value of the book for museums and collectors. Carl U. Fauster of the Antique and Historic Glass Foundation, Toledo, Ohio, and of The Glass Collectors Club of Toledo reviewed the manuscript and made many excellent suggestions. Janice H. Carlson, Museum Chemist, the Henry Francis du Pont Winterthur Museum, provided the X-ray fluorescence analysis of the Locke Art Glass pieces. Jane Shadel Spillman, Curator of American Glass, The Corning Museum of Glass, gave the manuscript an early critical reading, invited us to use the museum's library and wrote a foreword. Norma P. H. Jenkins, Head Librarian, and the staff of the Rakow Library at The Corning Museum of Glass provided invaluable assistance in research. John H. Martin, Deputy Director, The Corning Museum of Glass, offered overall publication suggestions and support. Bob and Edie Simonds supported us at critical stages and gave an excellent collectors' point of view. Robert Arnold, great-grandson of Joseph Locke, provided crucial photographic-printing assistance.

Introduction

Joseph Locke—the Artist

Joseph Locke (1846–1936)

JOSEPH LOCKE was born in Worcéster, England, on August 21, 1846. His father, Edward Locke, a potter, died when Joseph was a child, and Joseph was raised by his half brother Edward, a decorator and designer with the Royal Worcester China Factory.[1] Locke was apprenticed to the Royal Worcester Company when he was 12, and thus began his first, or English, career in the world of china and glass.

His career in the employ of major English glass houses lasted 24 years. During it, he became most noted for his glass sculpture and cameo glass. In 1882, when Locke was 36 years old, his fame was such that he was lured to the United States by the growing American glass community.

Joseph Locke's second career spanned the nine years he spent with Edward Drummond Libbey in Cambridge, Massachusetts, and in Toledo, Ohio. While working for Libbey, Locke developed processes for the manufacture of Amberina, Wild Rose (Peachblow), Pomona, Agata and Maize. These products are familiar to serious collectors of American art glass and are well documented in major American art-glass publications.

Locke's third career began after he left Libbey in about 1891 and moved to Pittsburgh, Pennsylvania, which was then an important glass center. For about ten years he worked as chief designer and consultant for the newly formed United States Glass Company. At the same time, he worked to perfect a process for the acid etching of glass that became the technology for Locke Art Glassware.

In 1898, at the age of 52, Locke established the Locke Art Glassware Company. Sometime between 1917 and 1920, when Locke was in his early seventies, the commercial nature of the business was phased out. Locke produced beautiful etched pieces as late as 1927, but not for commercial purposes. He died in 1936.

It is generally recognized that Joseph Locke was a master etcher of glass, and that in his later years he decorated high-quality glass blanks with exquisite florals and other designs from nature. Book and magazine treatments of the Locke Art Glassware period, Locke's most artistic, tend to regard it as the avocation of a retired man. In fact, Locke had children in public school at the time, and the business was the livelihood for his family for a 19-year period. It was terminated only when the various supporting members of the family moved on to other pursuits.

The literature on Joseph Locke also stresses some of the more dramatic museum-class pieces. It does not reflect the rich diversity of functional shapes, or the broad scope of the designs etched on the glass. It is the purpose of this volume to correct this situation, and to establish Locke's Pittsburgh career on a par with his earlier English and Libbey periods.

The English Period: 1858–1882

Locke's apprenticeship with Royal Worcester was an excellent one, and included instruction by leading English painters.[2] In this period, which lasted until he was about 19, he was also sent to study in Paris. Martha L. Rood quotes Locke's opinion of the "long-haired artists" that he had met there.[3] The lessons were effective, and his skill as an artist was evident at every step of his way to fame as an artist in glass.

At 19 Locke won a prize competition, sponsored by Guest Brothers, for the design of tiles for a fireplace to be built in a palace of the Czar. As a result, he jumped his apprenticeship at the Royal Worcester plant and joined Guest Brothers in Stourbridge. It was with Guest Brothers that he began to develop his skills in the decoration and etching of glass.[4]

Locke's children have claimed that their father, at that time, held both the amateur and professional English titles in the 100-yard dash. Through this activity he became friendly with William Hodgetts, of the firm of Hodgetts and Richardson in Wordsley, a suburb of Stourbridge. Hodgetts persuaded Locke to join his firm and start an etching-and-decorating plant. Hodgetts and Richardson became leaders in etched and engraved glass.[5] The company engaged a Frenchman, Alphonse-Eugène Lechevrel, to teach some of their men the process of engraving and cameo cutting on glass. Locke was his most apt pupil.[6]

Hodgetts and Richardson became committed to exhibiting at the Paris Exposition of 1878, and conceived the idea of having Joseph Locke reproduce the Portland Vase, using his cameo-cutting and engraving techniques.[7] Locke agreed, and the glassblowers made more than 30 blanks to allow for breakage caused by uneven expansion of the layers. Even with careful annealing over weeks, all but three "flew." The first of the remaining three blanks shattered during carving. The second survived the long period of carving and engraving and is still in perfect condition. Locke's copy helped to win a Paris Exposition Medal for Hodgetts and Richardson. It was exhibited in several cities throughout Great Britain[8] and was brought to the United States by Albert Christian Revi. The vase is currently in the collection of Dr. & Mrs. Leonard S. Rakow. (For a more complete understanding of the nineteenth-century interest in the reproduction of the Portland Vase, the significance of the original, and of ancient Roman cameo production, see the publications by Geoffrey Beard,[9] Albert Christian Revi[10] and Sidney M. Goldstein *et al.*[11] The point may be properly taken from these references that Joseph Locke was the peer of such famous nineteenth-century cameo artists as John Northwood I, Alphonse-Eugène Lechevrel, George Woodall and Frederick Carder.)

A disagreement developed between Locke and Richardson, and Locke moved to Pargeter and Company, but he did not get along with Mr. Pargeter and left to join Thomas Webb and Corbett. Joseph Edward (Ted) Locke, the elder son of Joseph, related that, at 12, he joined his father in the Pargeter plant, where Ted operated the etching machine. Ted was still with his father in the New England Glass Company in 1882, and in the Libbey plant in Toledo in 1888.[12] Throughout his career Locke continued this pattern of removing his sons from school to enter the glass business, citing his own education, which extended only through the fourth grade, as proof that one did not need formal education to work in the glass industry.

Locke was invited to come to America by the Boston and Sandwich Glass Company in 1882. He was scheduled to arrive in New York City, where the Boston and Sandwich people had gone to meet him. For some reason the ship landed in Boston, and the representative of Libbey's New England Glass Company got to him first. He began to work for them, probably in 1882.[13]

In his career with Libbey, Locke developed the processes for, and patented, Amberina, Pomona, Plated Amberina, Wild Rose (originally Peachblow), Agata and Maize.[14] Carl U. Fauster states that the survival of the New England Glass Company during its last years in Massachusetts was in part due to the art glass created by Joseph Locke. Libbey himself related how he avoided bankruptcy in 1883 by selling the factory's stock of Amberina to Tiffany & Co. in New York.[15]

We present here only short descriptions of these Joseph Locke/Libbey creations, our purpose being simply to establish Locke's stature in the field of American art glass. Excellent and complete descriptions and photographs of this glassware can be found in *Art Glass Nouveau*, by Ray and Lee Grover,[16] in *Nineteenth-Century Glass*, by Albert Christian Revi[17] and in *Libbey Glass Since 1818*, by Carl U. Fauster.[18]

Amberina

Amberina is a clear yellow glass that shades to red at the top. It is found in free-blown and mold-blown types.[19] The process was researched and patented by Joseph Locke in 1883, shortly after he came to America and joined with the New England Glass Company, which acquired the patent rights from Locke. The succeeding company, the Libbey Glass Company of Toledo, Ohio, marked a great number of pieces by etching the word "Libbey" on them. Amberina was imitated by several glass companies in the United States and Europe.[20]

The patent for Amberina, dated July 24, 1883, was granted to Joseph Locke, assignor to W. L. Libbey of Newton, and to Edward D. Libbey of Boston, Massachusetts. It was the first patented method for making shaded and particolored glass from a sensitive, homogeneous metal. A very small amount of gold, in solution, was colloidally dispersed in a transparent amber glass batch. Articles formed from this melt were first cooled below a glowing red heat, and then specified parts were reheated at the glory hole. This rapid cooling and reheating struck a red color in the reheated portion. The patent also provided for the development of shades of violet, green and blue, among others, through different reheating procedures.[21]

In addition to inventing the process for batching and reheating to create Amberina, Locke, as head designer of the Cambridge Works of the New England Glass Company, was also responsible for the design of pressed Amberina pieces.[22]

Plated Amberina

In 1886 Joseph Locke obtained a patent for Plated Amberina, which was made for a short time by the New England Glass Company at Cambridge.[23]

Wild Rose

In 1886 Edward Drummond Libbey obtained a patent for a glass now commonly known as Peachblow. The New England Glass Company's name for this product was Wild Rose. The Libbey Glass Company credits Joseph Locke with creating Wild Rose.[24]

Pomona

Under patents issued to Joseph Locke in 1885, the New England Glass Company in Cambridge produced this ware, of extreme delicacy, in practically every shape. The glass, clear at first, was subjected to a yellowish metallic stain and then fired around the upper border of the piece. The remainder of the glass consisted of an allover etching upon which was placed a small floral design of transparent metallic stain. The stain was frequently blue, as in the cornflower pattern, but is also found with a delicate enamel decoration, as in the blueberry pattern.[25]

References to Pomona mention "first grind" and "second grind," indicating the two manufacturing processes used. "First-grind" etching was accomplished by covering the glass with an acid-resistant coating into which were carved thousands of minute, overlapping circular engraved lines. Then acid was applied to eat into the glass where the lines had been carved. These lines may be seen with a low-power magnifying glass. Because the process was expensive, it was supplanted by the "second-grind" approach that was achieved by rolling the piece in very fine particles of acid-resistant material that adhered to the glass. When the piece was dipped into the acid a speckled acid etching resulted wherever there was no protection from the resistant particles. This "second-grind" is somewhat less brilliant in appearance.[26] Family members and others are becoming convinced that the term "grind" is a misnomer, and that the term is more correctly "ground," since it refers to the background area. The term was not used prior to the introduction of the second manufacturing process.

Agata

The New England Glass Company, Cambridge, produced Agata Glass under patents issued to Joseph Locke shortly after 1885. This glass consists of a metallic stain applied and fired on Wild Rose glass. Found in any Wild Rose shape, it appears as an allover pattern suggesting a fanciful spiderweb.[27]

Maize

Maize glass, also patented by Joseph Locke, was offered for sale by the W. L. Libbey and Sons Company, Toledo, Ohio, in 1889. This ware is a mold-blown glass with a glossy finish, except where maize (corn) leaves fan out from the foot. While these leaves are normally green, they are also found in red or blue.[28] Regis and Mary Ferson indicate that Maize items were mold-blown, most frequently in opaque white, but also in crystal and pale, opaque yellow. They report that the colored leaves are found in green, blue, rust, yellow or brown and are at times edged in gold.[29]

United States Glass Company Period, 1891–ca. 1898

For Joseph Locke the period between 1891 and 1898 was productive, but not in terms of art glass. He spent this time first in an abortive attempt to go into business on his own, and then as a designer and consultant with the newly formed United States Glass Company. Locke's contribution to the world of art glass during this period was indirect, and consisted of perfecting the patents for the manufacture of fire-resistant, reinforced glass. The money from the sale of these patent rights made it possible for him to enter into the business of making and selling Locke Art Glass.

Below is a list of dates and descriptions of glass-related patents that are technical rather than artistic. There is no evidence that Locke contributed any significant artistic designs to the product line of the United States Glass Company. Whereas Locke's Libbey-period patents were assigned to his company, it is interesting that these later ones were not assigned to the United States Glass Company.

Technical Patents Awarded to Joseph Locke, 1885–96

1885	Electrical insulator
1886	Apparatus for making and burning gaseous fuel
1894–95	Asbestos-covered wire glass
1894	Glass press
1894	Manufacture of hollowware
1894	Electrical insulator
1894	Method and apparatus for pressing glass
1895–96	Underground electrical conductor[30]

In this period Locke worked to perfect the technology of acid etching on crystal tableware that formed the process used by the Locke Art Glassware Company. The exact date of Locke's termination at the United States Glass Company is not known.

Locke Art Glassware Period, 1898–ca. 1920

Locke Art Glassware consisted of a full line of bon-bons, comports, fingerbowls, decanters, jugs, nappies, steins, stemware, tumblers, vases and small plates, all decorated by acid etching in a wide variety of designs including flowers, fruit, human figures, animals, birds, insects, trees and shrubs, as well as in numerous classic and stylized designs. These functional shapes and etched designs, shown in the original catalog, are reproduced here.

Locke Art Glassware is defined here as the glassware decorated by the Locke Art Glassware Company between 1898, the year in which the firm was founded, and ca. 1920, the approximate time at which it ceased to be a commercial venture. According to family members living in Locke's house at the time, orders were still being filled and shipped as late as 1919–20. Locke continued to decorate glass for his own satisfaction and for the delight of his family and friends, as late as 1927, when he was in his eighty-first year.

One way to determine whether or not a piece of glass is Locke Art Glassware is its inclusion in the catalog, which is evidence that the piece was produced for sale. A second means of identification is the presence of the Locke Art or Jo Locke signature on a piece. Some articles, particularly smaller ones such as wines and liqueurs, do not bear a signature. To determine whether such items are Locke Art Glassware, it is necessary to compare them either with a picture in the catalog or with a piece that bears the signature. The shape of the glassware and the standard etched decorations are readily matched in this manner.

In a recent study of 244 pieces of Locke Art Glass, each one different, 59 pieces were found lacking the usual Locke Art or Jo Locke signature. Seven of these pieces were not of the classic floral or fruit genres. The remaining 52 pieces, clearly in the Locke Art Glassware tradition, were not signed. Many of these are displayed in the Locke Art Glassware catalog. Some of them are set mates to signed pieces. It is our opinion, supported by other family members, that it was through simple oversight that these pieces were not signed. It is clear that, in the process of decorating Locke Art Glass, the signature was applied to the resist early in the process, at the same time as all other "bright" lines, including the main outlines of the fruits or flowers. Signatures that were omitted at this stage could not be inscribed later. Our survey indicates that the lack of a signature can be expected one out of five times, on a random basis, probably because of poor quality control. The Locke Art signature and the paper sticker trademark applied prior to shipping are reproduced here, both enlarged.

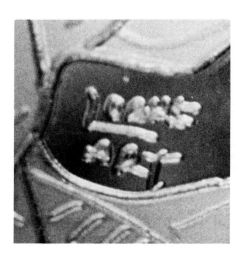 

The glassware shown in this catalog was produced by an acid-etching process perfected by Joseph Locke. High-quality crystal blanks, most imported from Austria and Belgium, were first coated with a resist. The lines and areas to be etched were inscribed on the glass, which was then exposed to the acid. At least two separate removals and exposures were required to achieve both the bright line and the frosted effects. In some cases, such as with grape and cherry patterns, highlights were created by buffing with a cork wheel.

The concrete foundation of the shop at the rear of 442 Carl Street in Mt. Oliver, in Pittsburgh, now supports a three-car garage with a 15' × 20' storage area on the first floor and a fair-sized dwelling on the second. The original shop, of wooden construction, burned, probably in 1912–13, and was replaced by one of brick. Both were one-story. It is believed that no more than four or five people were employed there at any time.

The Etched Design

The photographs from the original catalog reproduced here did not include the names of the etched designs available or shown. The customer would select the etched design desired from the pictures or from the samples carried by the salesman. The names used here are taken from a sales-order book that records the sales made in a six-month period in 1906–07. In those cases in which the name of the design has not been shown in the sales-order book, an appropriate name has been created by the authors. The created names are marked by an asterisk.

The most popular etched design sold in this period was Grape or Grape & Lines, which accounted for 48 percent of all pieces sold.[31] Daisy, Rose, Ivy, Thistle, Violet, Poppy and Forget-Me-Not made up 42 percent. Fruits were the next most popular class of decoration. Strawberries, Currants, Berries, Cherries and a beautiful Pineapple & Grape design make up little more than five percent of the designs ordered.

The etched flower and fruit decorations applied by Locke have been examined by the staff of the Hunt Institute for Botanical Documentation, Carnegie-Mellon University, who have concluded that Locke was an excellent student of botany.

Two patterns deserve special mention. The design that Locke called Egyptian (page 49) has been researched by the Fine Arts Department of the University of Pittsburgh. They have agreed that the figure shown is the Egyptian goddess Nut, who is generally shown with falcon wings and with a pot on her head. The pitcher in this set sold for $50 and the goblets for $120 a dozen.

The second set of this quality is the Uncle Remus series, which came with a pitcher and with a dozen goblets, each one showing a different situation from the Uncle Remus stories of Joel Chandler Harris (p. 19).[32]

The list on the top of page 11 represents all design subjects created by Locke for etching into the glass that are known to the authors. The artist's interest in flowers and his skill in depicting them dated back to his apprentice days in England. The first eight flowers and plants listed are in order of customer preference, as reflected in the sales record of 1906–07. The remaining 19 flower and plant designs have been identified from the original sales catalog and from a personal survey of 11 major Locke Art Glassware collections made during 1985–86.

If our calculations are right, more than 75 percent of the etched pieces were done entirely freehand. At the same time, however, the freehand pieces maintained an amazing consistency of layout and detail. The authors have conducted a close analysis of the Grape & Lines tumbler in all 11 collections reviewed. This represents the most popular piece made commercially by Locke. Each contains the following major elements that have been applied to the tumbler in the sequence listed: lines, major leaves, major horizontal stem bundles, grape clusters and remaining minor leaves, stems and tendrils. Although the individual grape clusters and the related stems, leaves and

Flowers and Plants		People	Fruits
daisy	poinsettia	ballerina	grape
rose	primrose	woman at churn	strawberry
wild rose	rye grass	woman of fashion	raspberry
poppy	shamrock	sweethearts	cherry
ivy			currant
thistle	*Poultry*	*Antiquity*	pineapple
violet	*Butterflies*	Egyptian goddess	lemon
water lily	*Symbols and Designs*	(Nut)	orange
anemone	crescent	Greco-Roman	
carnation	coat of arms	figures	*Religion*
chrysanthemum	fleur-de-lis		Joseph and Mary
clematis	Masonic symbol	*Animals*	Rebecca at the
cosmos	basket of flowers	horse	well
cyclamen	garlands	deer	
daffodil		elk	*Arts and Literature*
fern	*Sports*	dog	Hiawatha
forget-me-not	horseman	fox	Alice in
fuchsia	horsewoman	rabbit	Wonderland
iris	polo		Brer Rabbit
juniper berry	golfing	*Fish and Shellfish*	Wagner operas
lady's slipper	canoeing	game fish	Kewpie doll
morning glory	hunting	lobster	Cupid
nasturtium	tennis	oyster	
orchid	yachting		
	sailboating		

tendrils are each different, both on a single tumbler and on each tumbler of a ⟨   ⟩ he general layout of the elements is completely consistent, a feature found in ⟨   ⟩ Locke's popular patterns, indicating that once Locke achieved a good design, he ⟨   ⟩ not deviate from it.

Fruit is the second most important category of design. Grape is by far the mos⟨ ⟩ often found, followed by Strawberry, Raspberry, Cherry, Currant and Pineapple.

As Locke's subject moved into the realms of animals, sports, religion, antiquity, arts and literature, the product seemed to change from artistic repetitive reproduction to artistic creation. In addition to the Brer Rabbit and Egyptian designs mentioned above, the Silverman article refers to characters from Wagner's operas, Rebecca at the Well, the Good Shepherd, and a piece called Encore, inspired by Adelina Patti.[33] Many of these pieces clearly constitute unique works of art, and are Locke Art Glassware only in the sense that Locke created them using the same etching techniques and, in many cases, signed them with the Locke Art signature.

By personal analysis of over 500 pieces, and by considered discussions with older cousins who saw the shop in operation, we have come to the conclusion that Joseph Locke personally did the primary bright-line artwork on all of the freehand pieces and that he probably did the work on some of the 15 to 20 percent of the pieces that were done using a copper template.

Silverman, who personally interviewed Joseph Locke and several of Locke's children, reported that daughter May and son Frank did some of the "conventional" pieces (described below). The function of other children, and of neighborhood women who were known to have worked in the shop, doubtless included the removal of the resist from the areas of the design that were to be given the second, matte finish. They also did the final removal of the resist from the glassware, in what the grandchildren have called the "bosh" process. It is also possible that other people operated the machines for inscribing the bright lines on the coated piece and for using the cork wheel to buff the highlights onto the grapes and cherries. The author's father, T. Hubert (Bert) Locke, has stated that he did much of the acid work. Bert Locke was also secretary/treasurer of the company and its chief sales representative for many years.

The consistency of style and detail of specific popular patterns found in all collections reviewed in the 1985–86 survey present the strongest argument that Locke was the sole artist for all of the freehand work. A review of production for a six-month period in 1906–07 shows that the daily figures had to be between 12 and 15 pieces a day, a task well within the capabilities of a single artist.

Of the 143 glass shapes displayed in the Locke Art Glassware catalog, 27 percent were offered in both a freehand and a "conventional" line. Pieces listed as "conventional" were available, in certain etched designs, at a price of 50 to 80 percent of the freehand price. The factors that entered into the decision to offer a given piece in both a freehand and a "conventional" line certainly related to its shape, and probably also to the use and price of the piece. Only a few of the larger pieces are offered "in conv.," and in these cases only in the most popular No. 33–line pieces. Also, extensive fluting and recurving of the piece seemed to militate against the use of a template. Since the original catalog relates only the "conventional" option to the shape of the glass piece, the salesman must have had another source that indicated which etched designs were available for each piece. Only four of the 38 pieces indicated in the catalog as available "in conv." appear from the pictures to have been created with a template.

It is possible to tell if a piece has been made with the use of a template by examination of the stem line and blossom. Template use in each case will result in a double-line stem, while freehand drawn stems will show a single line. However, in some large patterns, the stem was drawn freehand and double, but in a fashion different from the traced variety (*see* No. 1125, five-pint pitcher, p. 47). In these cases, the blossom must be examined. On "conventional" pieces, the blossom will be of standard outline on the three or four repetitions. This will be true both on a single piece, and on each of its pieces of a set. It is estimated that after the basic outline of the stems and flower were done, another ten to 20 percent of freehand work was required to complete the artwork on the piece. Joseph Locke may well have personally done this finishing work, judging from the consistency of execution.

Whether for reasons of production or of customer preference, the "conventional" option was not used extensively. Of the 1872 pieces ordered in the six-month period in 1905–06, none were ordered "in conv." Of the 244 different shapes and designs examined by the authors in 1985–86, only 27 were decorated in the "conventional" fashion. Although, overall, "conventional" pieces probably represent less than 15 percent of the total production, from a collector's point of view, they represent a significant variation. In the 27 "conventional" pieces recently examined, Poppy was the most frequently found (17), and Rose was next (5). There were two Poinsettia and one each of Iris, Strawberry and Nasturtium. In every case the "conventional," or template, production piece was signed with the Locke Art signature.

Illustrated here is an example of the Rose template, with a photograph of a Rose pattern on a goblet showing the amount of detail in the template and the additional handwork that was done. Also shown is an example of freehand Rose.

Rose template

Rose goblet (conventional)

Freehand Rose goblet

The acid etching of glass had been perfected in many English and American glass-houses in the 1870s.[34] Except for Locke's work, however, it was not developed as an independent art, but was an imitation of cutting.[35] Acid etching of glass had been practiced in England long before the 1870s and Joseph Locke was known to have been employed, both in England and by Libbey, in etching operations.

Locke experimented constantly with resists to solve different problems, including the effects of varying weather conditions. He worked with beeswax, paraffin, stearin and mutton fat and with various solvents and gums. He knew that highly concentrated hydrofluoric acid would produce deep, bright etchings and that the addition of ammonium carbonate and various salts gave gradations in the etch from bright, through satin, to a dense matte. He frequently applied thickened acid with a brush to fill the spaces between deep-line etches.[36] It is clear from examination of etched pieces that Locke consistently used two successive exposures to different acid solutions, each exposure involving additional resist removal.

The distinguishing characteristic of Locke Art Glassware etching is this use of two layers of etching, which makes part of the design appear in relief. The edge of the leaf or the outline of the pattern will be more pronounced than the rest of the design.[37] The "bright" lines are deeply etched and do not show any frosted effect. In each case a large portion of the design shows a frosted or a matte finish. This is generally in areas of leaf or blossom or in large areas such as human or animal figures.

On designs of smooth-skinned fruit, such as grapes and cherries, the fruit area was first outlined in "bright" lines. It was removed from the acid bath, and the inside areas were scraped clean and exposed to another, "frosting" acid. Grape, cherry or similar smooth-skinned fruit were then buffed by a cork wheel to provide a highlight. On berries and strawberries the texture and detail of the skin is clearly applied free-hand (*see* Strawberry, p. 39).

From time to time Locke deviated from his normal practice of frosting the areas of a flower or fruit, and applied a finish similar to "first-grind" Pomona. This is most notable in the Lemon and the Orange designs. Several pieces have been found that show the Pomona-type finish as a general background to a clear floral design.

Alexander Silverman reported that the fire in the shop at 442 Carl Street destroyed most of the records of formulas of resists, etching fluids and processes. He felt that Locke did not record them again after the fire.[38]

The Glassware

The name of the specific piece of glass illustrated is provided on the facing page in the same relative position on the page as the glass, at the head of each set of descriptive information. This name is taken directly from the original catalog prepared by Locke. In cases where it was not included, the authors have created the name.

The third line in each set also pertains to the glassware. Where the number of the glass blank is known, it is listed, followed by the size of the piece or its volume. You will note, for instance, that the saucer-footed sherbet (p. 21) is shown in shapes No. 41, No. 42 and No. 1. Note, also, that the No. 1 saucer-footed sherbet is part of the complete No. 1–line stemware set shown on page 29 in the Shamrock pattern. The No. 50 footed bon-bon, shown on page 37, came in five-inch or six-inch sizes. Also, the decanter No. 44, shown on page 43, also in the Shamrock pattern, was available in two-pint, one-pint and half-pint capacities.

Locke family members recall that Joseph Locke preferred to work with glass from Belgium or Austria and that he was unable to find a domestic supplier who could meet his needs. Effort is being made to determine the European and domestic sources of the glassware used by Locke. Family members have reported that Locke frequently purchased small quantities of domestic glass for decoration and sale, and that domestic suppliers provided him with sample pieces to try. They have also stated Locke's claim that each kind of glass called for its own set of resist and acid-etching conditions.

Two of the types of glass Locke purchased most frequently have been taken to the Henry Francis du Pont Winterthur Museum near Wilmington, Delaware, where they have been subjected to quantitative energy-dispersive X-ray–fluorescence analysis. The following values were considered meaningful:

CONCENTRATION (Wt. %)

Element	Tumbler, base	Sherbet, foot	Sherbet, side
Lead	5.5	8.1	7.8
Potassium	3.8	.18	.21
Calcium	1.4	.73	.81

The glass used in these objects is unusual in that the lead content is significantly less than the 30 to 40 percent usually found in the nineteenth- and twentieth-century lead glass.[39]

Optic

Some Locke pieces could be ordered in "optic" style, which was a standard technique in tableware factories. Optic-molded pieces appear to have a molded pattern, such as roundels or ribs, but the pattern cannot be felt on the exterior surface. To produce this effect, a piece is first mold-blown in a mold cut with the desired pattern. Then it is placed in a mold which conforms to the desired shape but is unpatterned, and is blown again. The second blowing smooths the outer surface and pushes the pattern to the inside, where it can be felt on the surface.

Locke had three popular pieces that were available with and without the "optic" feature: the No. 33 pitcher, the No. 1 goblet and the No. 10 tumbler. Examination of the 1906–07 sales-order book shows at least 20 instances in which the No. 33 pitcher was ordered with the No. 1 goblet, or the No. 10 tumbler. In each case the order indicated consistently that the total set should be either "optic" or not, according to the wishes of the customer.

Four other shapes are known to be "optic" by inspection. For these pieces the order book does not specify "optic." The conclusion is that the shape came only in "optic." These are: No. 3 tumbler (p. 17), No. 41 saucer-footed sherbet (p. 21), No. 42 saucer-footed sherbet (p. 21) and No. 24 grapefruit (p. 39).

Price and Value

The retail prices for most pieces are shown in the original catalog, and are shown here in the fourth line of each set of information on the pages facing the illustrations.

The prices shown in this reproduction of the original Locke Art Glassware catalog represent the cost to the customer. The following are representative prices contrasted with the price from the 1906–07 sales-order book. It is clear that the china shop or jewelry store enjoyed a 100 percent markup, and that the catalog was used by the salesman when demonstrating product and price to the ultimate customer.

Piece Description	Sales Catalog	Sales-order Book
No. 10 Tumbler	$14.00 doz.	$6.40 doz.
No. 1 Goblet	$24.00 doz.	$12.00 doz.
No. 33 Pitcher	$13.00 ea.	$6.50 ea.
No. 83 Comport	$8.00 ea.	$3.65 ea.
No. 33 Sugar and Creamer	$9.00 set	$4.50 set
No. 41 Saucer-footed Sherbet	$16.00 doz.	$8.00 doz.

The quality of the glass used by Locke and the artistry and excellence of the etched decoration placed Locke Art Glassware in a class with the best cut crystal available at the time. This is evident from the following table, comparing the retail price of the etched crystal of Joseph Locke with that of some of the most expensive cut crystal from Libbey of Toledo,[40] Higgins & Seiter of New York[41] and John Wanamaker of Philadelphia.[42]

	Libbey (1905)	Higgins & Seiter (1905)	John Wanamaker (1880)	Locke Art Glassware (1900)
Tumblers (Dozen)	$16.00–$36.00	$12.00–$27.00	$12.00–$20.00	$14.00–$120.00
Goblets (Dozen)	$40.00–$52.00	$15.75–$36.50	$12.00–$25.00	$24.00–$125.00
Champagne (Dozen)	$36.00–$48.00	$15.75–$28.50	$12.00–$20.00	$24.00
Decanter (Pair)	$24.00	$10.00–$30.00	$ 7.00–$20.00	$14.00

The following quotation, repeated from the Preface, stands beside the above "dollars-and-cents" testimony to the artistry and value of Locke Art Glassware: "beautiful masterpieces in glassware . . . each individual piece a work of art surpassing, the best results of Bohemian and French glassmakers." The quote takes on more meaning when the "glassmen" at the meeting are named: A. H. Heisey, two of the Gillanders of Gillander and Sons, E. P. Ebberts of Phoenix Glass, M. W. Gleason for C. Dorflinger and Sons, and others.[43]

By these tokens, Locke Art Glass was recognized as an art glass of exceptional merit on a national and an international basis.

Notes

1. Alexander Silverman, "Joseph Locke, Artist," *The Glass Industry*, vol. 17, no. 8, 1936, pp. 1–2.
2. *Ibid.*, p. 2.
3. Martha L. Rood, "One of Pittsburgh's Real Artists," *The Index* (Pittsburgh), July 8, 1916.
4. Silverman, *op. cit.*, p. 2.
5. *Ibid.*, p. 4.
6. Nell Jaffe Baer, "Joseph Locke and His Art Glass," *Auction* (Parke Bernet Galleries), vol. 11, no. 8, reproduction p. 1, April 1969, p. 9.
7. Silverman, *op. cit.*, p. 6.
8. Albert C. Revi, *Nineteenth-Century Glass* (New York: Thomas Nelson and Sons, 1967), p. 149.
9. Geoffrey W. Beard, *Nineteenth-Century Cameo Glass* (Newport, Monmouthshire, England: Ceramic Book Company, 1956), pp. 1–27, 60–62.
10. Revi, *op. cit.*, pp. 135–161.
11. Sidney M. Goldstein, Leonard S. Rakow, Juliette K. Rakow, *Cameo Glass: Masterpieces from 2000 Years of Glassmaking* (Corning, New York: The Corning Museum of Glass, 1982), pp. 8–29.
12. *Toledo Daily Blade*, August 18, 1888. (Reprinted in Fauster, *Libbey Glass Since 1818*, pp. 35–36.)
13. Silverman, *op. cit.*, p. 7.
14. Carl U. Fauster, *Libbey Glass Since 1818* (Toledo, Ohio: Len Beach Press, 1979), p. 34.
15. *Ibid.*, p. 25.
16. Ray Grover and Lee Grover, *Art Glass Nouveau* (Rutland, Vermont: Charles E. Tuttle Company, 1967), pp. 40–54.
17. Revi, *op. cit.*, pp. 2–60.
18. Fauster, *op. cit.*, pp. 25–59, 169–197, 225–227; Figs. 21–28, 30–33, 53.
19. Grover, *op. cit.*, p. 17.
20. *Ibid.*
21. Revi, *op. cit.*, pp. 16, 17.
22. *Ibid.*, p. 23.
23. Grover, *op. cit.*, p. 18.
24. *Libbey Glass: A Tradition of 150 Years* (Toledo, Ohio: The Toledo Museum of Art, 1968), p. 26.
25. Grover, *op. cit.*, p. 54.
26. *Ibid.*, p. 55.
27. *Ibid.*, p. 51.
28. *Ibid.*, pp. 219, 220.
29. Regis Ferson and Mary Fleming Ferson, *Yesterday's Milk Glass Today* (Pittsburgh, Pennsylvania: Regis and Mary Ferson, Publishers, 1981), p. 489.
30. Silverman, *op. cit.*, p. 11.
31. Joseph H. Locke and Jane T. Locke, "Locke Art Glassware: Its Functional Shapes and Etched Designs," *Hobbies*, January 1985, vol. 89, no. 11, p. 28.
32. Joel Chandler Harris, *Tales from Uncle Remus* (New York, New York: Black Heritage Library Collection, Arno Press, Inc.). (Reprint of the illustrated 1905 edition.)
33. Silverman, *op. cit.*, p. 10.
34. Carl W. Dreppard, *A.B.C.s of Old Glass* (Garden City, New York: Doubleday and Company, Inc., 1949), p. 29.
35. Dorothy Daniel, *Cut and Engraved Glass: 1771–1905* (New York: M. Barrows and Company, Inc., 1971), p. 64.
36. Silverman, *op. cit.*, p. 2.
37. Daniel, *op. cit.*, p. 70.
38. Silverman, *op. cit.*, p. 7.
39. Winterthur Museum Analytical Laboratory, Wilmington, Delaware; "Report No. 1593, 7/27/84," by Janice H. Carlson.
40. Fauster, *op. cit.*, pp. 254–286.
41. Higgins & Seiter, Inc., *Rich Cut Glass and Fine China* (New York, ca. 1905).
42. John Wanamaker, *Catalog of Crockery and China* (Philadelphia, ca. 1880).
43. *The Crockery and Glass Journal*, July 20, 1905, p. 24.

Joseph Locke, Pres.   *F. Hubert Locke, Secy & Tr*

Locke Art Glassware Company
Designers & Decorators of Fine Glassware
442 Carl St., Mt. Oliver Sta., Pittsburgh, Pa.

TUMBLER				
Grape & Lines	Fuchsia*	Rose	Violet & Lines	Grape & Lines
No. 3, 11 oz.	No. 10, 8 oz.	No. 10, 8 oz.	No. 10, 8 oz.	No. 26, 9 oz.
$16.00 doz.	$14.00 doz.	$14.00 doz.	$14.00 doz.	$14.00 doz.

TUMBLER		
Thistle	Thistle	Thistle
No. 3, 3 oz.	No. 3, 11 oz.	No. 3, 3 oz.
$6.00 doz.	$16.00 doz.	$6.00 doz.

Decoration names marked with "" do not appear in the original catalog or sales-order book and have been created by the authors.

TUMBLER, SET OF TWELVE
Brer Rabbit No. 10, 8 oz., 12 oz. $120.00 doz.

TUMBLER				
Ivy	Fish	Grape & Lines	Lemon*	Fuchsia*

TUMBLER-WHISKEY			
Grape & Lines No. 3, 3 oz. $12.00 doz.	Thistle No. 3, 2 oz. $12.00 doz.	Wheat* No. 3, 2 oz. $12.00 doz.	Juniper Berry* No. 20, 1 oz. $12.00 doz.

*Name created by the authors.

SAUCER-FOOTED SHERBET OR ICE		
Grape & Lines No. 41 $24.00 doz.	Three Fruit No. 41 $24.00 doz.	Daisy No. 41 $16.00 doz.

SAUCER-FOOTED SHERBET OR ICE		
Rose No. 1 $24.00 doz.	Fern* No. 42 $24.00 doz.	Daisy No. 1 $16.00 doz.

OYSTER COCKTAIL OR EGG	SAUCER-FOOTED SHERBET OR ICE		OYSTER COCKTAIL OR EGG	
Oyster No. 1	Ivy No. 41 $16.00 doz.	Forget-Me-Not No. 1 $10.00 doz.	Chicken & Egg* No. 2 $16.00 doz.	Fish No. 1 $30.00 doz.
SAUCER-FOOTED SHERBET OR ICE				
Rose No. 41 $24.00 doz.	Forget-Me-Not No. 42	Grecian (anthemion) No. 1	Grecian No. 41	Grecian No. 42

*Name created by the authors.

GOBLET			
Daisy No. 1 $16.00 doz.	Grape & Lines No. 1 $24.00 doz.	Rose No. 2 $24.00 doz.	Rose No. 1 $24.00 doz.

TALL CHAMPAGNE	GOBLET	TALL CHAMPAGNE	GOBLET	TALL CHAMPAGNE	CUT-STEM GOBLET	TALL CHAMPAGNE
Forget-Me-Not No. 1	Grape No. 2 $24.00 doz.	Thistle & Crown* No. 1	Forget-Me-Not No. 1	Rose No. 1	Rose	Grape & Lines No. 1

*Name created by the authors.

CUT-STEM GOBLET	SHORT-STEM GOBLET	FOOTED TUMBLER	SHORT-STEM GOBLET
Cyclamen No. 24 $36.00 doz.	Rose No. 1 $24.00 doz.	Oyster No. 1 $16.00 doz.	Rose No. 24 $24.00 doz.

	FOOTED TUMBLER		CUT-STEM GOBLET
Thistle No. 1, Coat of Arms $16.00 doz.	Grape & Lines No. 1 $16.00 doz.	Forget-Me-Not No. 1, Monogram $16.00 doz.	Rose No. 24 $36.00 doz.

FOOTED TUMBLER		CUT-STEM GOBLET	FOOTED TUMBLER	TUMBLER
Cyclamen No. 1	Grape No. 1	Cyclamen No. 24	Rose No. 1	Oak Leaf & Acorn*

*Name created by the authors.

OYSTER COCKTAIL OR EGG
Set of Twelve Different Fishes
No. 1
$48.00 set of 12

PARFAIT
Grape
No. 1
$20.00 doz.

OYSTER COCKTAIL OR EGG			
Oyster	Chicken & Egg*	Clematis*	Ivy
No. 1	No. 2	No. 2	No. 3
$16.00 doz.	$16.00 doz.	$16.00 doz.	$16.00 doz.

*Name created by the authors.

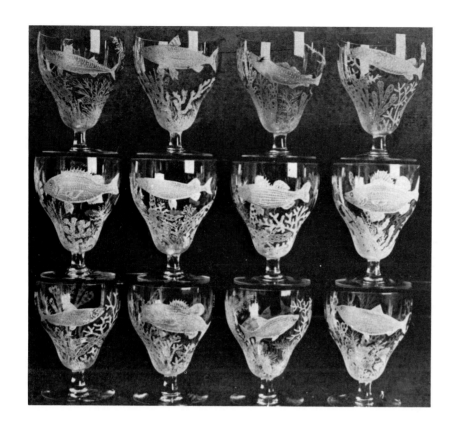

CORDIAL	SAUCER-FOOTED SHERBET OR ICE	FINGERBOWL	WINE	CRÈME DE MENTHE OR COCKTAIL
Shamrock No. 1, 1 oz. $18.00 doz.	Shamrock No. 1 $24.00 doz.	Shamrock No. 1 $30.00 doz.	Shamrock No. 1, 3 oz. $19.20 doz.	Shamrock No. 1 $18.00 doz.

bottom row, left

TALL CORDIAL	SHERRIE**	TUMBLER	CLARET
Shamrock No. 1 $18.00 doz.	Shamrock No. 1 $18.00 doz.	Shamrock No. 1, 8 oz., 12 oz. $14.00, $16.00 doz.	Shamrock No. 1, 4 oz. $19.20 doz.

bottom row, right

GOBLET	TALL CHAMPAGNE	SAUCER CHAMPAGNE STEM SHERBET	OYSTER COCKTAIL OR EGG
Shamrock $24.00 doz	Shamrock $24.00 doz.	Shamrock $24.00 doz.	Shamrock $19.20 doz.

PORT*	SHERRIE*	CLARET*	RHINE WINE*	MOSELLE WINE*	CORDIAL*
Violet	Violet	Violet	Violet	Violet	Violet

COCKTAIL*	SHERBET*	GOBLET*	CHAMPAGNE*	FINGERBOWL*
Violet	Violet	Violet	Violet	Violet

*Name created by the authors.
**Original spelling.

CLARET	SHERRIE	COCKTAIL OR CRÈME DE MENTHE
Grape & Lines No. 1, 4 oz. $19.20 doz.	Grape & Lines No. 1, 3 oz. $19.20 doz.	Rooster & Cherries No. 1 $19.20 doz.

SHERRIE		FINGERBOWL		WHITE WINE
Cresent* cut teardrop stem		Cresent*		Cresent* cut teardrop stem

PORT	TALL CHAMPAGNE	GOBLET	SAUCER CHAMPAGNE OR STEM SHERBET	CLARET
Cresent* cut teardrop stem	Cresent* cut teardrop stem	Cresent* cut teardrop stem	Cresent* cut teardrop stem	Cresent* cut teardrop stem

*Name created by the authors.

STEIN		
Canoeist* No. 16 $30.00 doz.	Grape No. 16 $30.00 doz.	Baseball Catcher* No. 16 $30.00 doz.

STEIN			
Hunter & Dog* No. 16 $30.00 doz.	Polo* No. 16 $30.00 doz.	Antlered Deer* No. 16 $30.00 doz.	Horse & Rider* No. 16 $30.00 doz.

STEIN		
Violet No. 16 $30.00 doz.	Fuchsia* No. 16 $30.00 doz.	Rose No. 16 $30.00 doz.

STEIN			
Grape No. 17 $30.00 doz.	Rose No. 17 $30.00 doz.	Woman at Churn* No. 17 $30.00 doz.	Oak Leaf & Acorn* No. 17 $30.00 doz.

*Name created by the authors.

STEIN			
Golfer* No. 16 $30.00 doz.	Sailboat* No. 16 $30.00 doz.	B.P.O.E. Elks* No. 16 $30.00 doz.	Baseball Thrower* No. 16 $30.00 doz.

STEIN			
Hunting Dog* No. 16 $30.00 doz.	Tennis Woman* No. 16 $30.00 doz.	Woman Golfer* No. 16 $30.00 doz.	Fisherman* No. 16 $30.00 doz.

FINGERBOWL			
Berry No. 20 $30.00 doz.	Rose No. 22 $30.00 doz.	Lace & Lines* No. 1 $30.00 doz.	Cyclamen No. 1 $30.00 doz.

FINGERBOWL			
Clematis* No. 21 $30.00 doz.	Fish No. 1 $30.00 doz.	Grape No. 23 $30.00 doz.	Forget-Me-Not No. 1 $30.00 doz.

FINGERBOWL		
Butterfly & Wheat* No. 1 $30.00 doz.	Rose No. 1 $30.00 doz.	Water Lily* No. 1 $30.00 doz.

*Name created by the authors.

FOOTED BON-BON		
Grape	Currant (Gooseberry)	Poppy
No. 1	No. 50, 5 in., 6 in.	No. 1
$30.00 doz.	$30.00, $36.00 doz.	$30.00 doz.

FOOTED BON-BON		
Rose	Grape	Poppy
No. 50, 5 in., 6 in.	No. 50, 5 in., 6 in.	No. 50, 5 in., 6 in.
$1.50, $2.00 ea.	$1.50, $2.00 ea.	$1.50, $2.00 ea.

(saucer)	FOOTED BON-BON		(saucer)
Indian Almond	Indian Almond	Indian Almond	Indian Almond
3 in.	No. 50, 5 in.	No. 1, 5 in.	3 in.
$14.00 doz.	$30.00 doz.	$30.00 doz.	$14.00 doz.

BON-BON		
Rose	Grape	Morning Glory*
No. 3, 5 in.	No. 3, 5 in.	No. 3, 5 in.
$3.00 ea.	$3.00 ea.	$3.00 ea.

NAPPIE**	
Berry & Strawberry	Berry & Strawberry
No. 33, 6 in.	No. 33, 9 in.
$30.00 doz.	$8.00 ea.

GRAPEFRUIT	
Strawberry	Grape
No. 24	No. 3
$40.00 doz.	$42.00 doz.

*Name created by the authors.
**Original spelling.

COMPORT**	FOOTED COMPORT**
Rose No. 83 $13.00 ea.	Pineapple & Grape No. 1, 9 in. $13.00 ea.

COMPORT**			
			Rose
No. 78 $9.00 ea.	No. 79 $9.00 ea.	No. 80 $9.00 ea.	No. 81 $9.00 ea.

COMPORT**	VASE	COMPORT**
Grecian No. 79 $9.00	Grape & Lines 8½ in.	Rose No. 78, 9½ in. $9.00

**Original spelling.

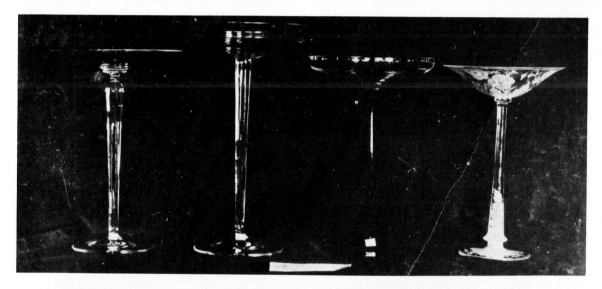

SHERRIE WINE	DECANTER	SHERRIE WINE
Berry	Berry (Monogram)	Berry (Monogram)
No. 2	No. 20, 2 pt., 1 pt.	No. 2
$18.00 doz.	$8.00, $6.00 ea.	$18.00 doz.

DECANTER	SHERRIE WINE	DECANTER	CORDIAL	TALL CORDIAL	DECANTER	WHISKEY
Shamrock	Shamrock	Shamrock	Shamrock	Shamrock	Shamrock	Shamrock
No. 44, 2 pt.	No. 1	No. 44, 1 pt.	No. 1	No. 1	No. 44, ½ pt.	No. 1
$8.00 ea.	$18.00 doz.	$6.00 ea.	$10.00 doz.	$18.00 doz.	$6.00 ea.	$12.00 doz.

		DECANTER	LOVING CUP (three-handled)
DECANTER			
Berry	Berry	Rose (wild)	Rose

CRÈME DE MENTHE OR COCKTAIL	DECANTER	CRÈME DE MENTHE OR COCKTAIL
Shamrock	Shamrock	Shamrock
No. 1	No. 46, 1 pt., 2 pt.	No. 1
$18.00 doz.	$6.00, $8.00 ea.	$18.00 doz.

PITCHER	GOBLET	PITCHER
Grape & Lines No. 1125 $40.00 ea.	Grape No. 2	Grape No. 1125

PITCHER	PITCHER
Hiawatha* No. 1125 $50.00 ea.	Horses & Riders* No. 1125

*Name created by the authors.

PITCHER	PITCHER
Rose No. 33, 5 pt., 3 pt., 1 pt. $14.00, $13.00, $6.00 ea.	Grape & Lines No. 33, 5 pt., 3 pt., 1 pt. $14.00, $13.00, $6.00 ea.

GOBLET	TANKARD†	TUMBLER	TANKARD†
Egyptian No. 2 $120.00 doz.	Egyptian No. 50 $50.00 ea.	Ivy	Ivy No. 50

†Although the original catalog identifies these pieces as tankards, their lips would indicate that they were actually pitchers.

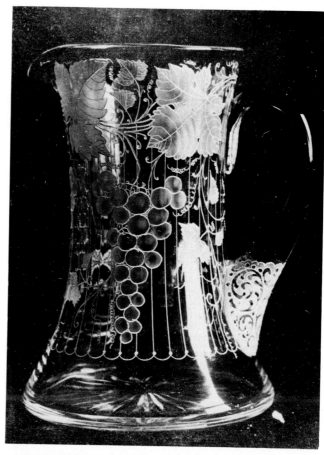

PITCHER	TUMBLER	PITCHER
Rose & Lines	Rose & Lines	Sweethearts

PITCHER		
Woman Golfer*	Woman with Flute*	Wild Rose & Lines*

*Name created by the authors.

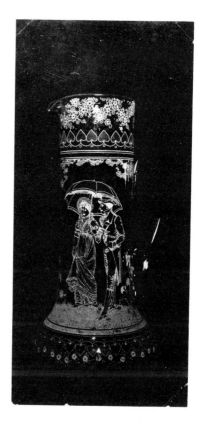

WATER BOTTLE		
Poppy	Water Lily* (with tumbler)	Grape
		$8.00 ea.

SUGAR AND CREAMER
Grape & Lines (with monogram) No. 33 $9.00 set

*Name created by the authors.

VASE	VASE	VASE
Primrose* No. 64, 12 in. $10.00 ea.	Lady's Slipper* No. 64, 12 in. $10.00 ea.	Morning Glory* No. 64, 12 in. $10.00 ea.

SWEET PEA VASE		
No. 35, #3, 10 in. $9.00 ea.	No. 35, #2, 8 in. $7.00 ea.	Rose No. 35, #1 $5.00 ea.

*Name created by the authors.

  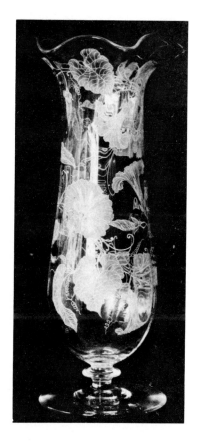

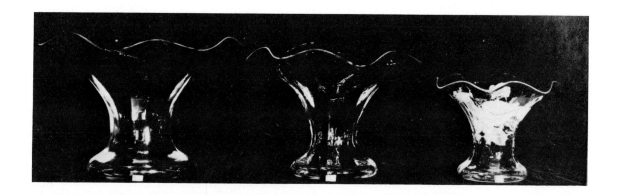

TWO-HANDLED VASE		
Grape & Lines No. 33, 8 in. $6.50 ea.	Grape & Lines No. 33, 10 in. $10.00 ea.	Grape & Lines No. 33, 6 in. $4.50 ea.

VASE		
Iris* No. 21, 7 in. $3.00 ea.	Butterfly & Wheat* No. 12 $3.00 ea.	Lady's Slipper No. 19 $2.50 ea.

*Name created by the authors.

VASE	VASE
Berry No. 61, 12 in., 8 in. $10.00, $6.00 ea.	Rose No. 61, 12 in., 8 in. $10.00, $6.00 ea.

TWO-HANDLED VASE	TWO-HANDLED VASE
Cupid* No. 33, 10 in., 8 in., 6 in.	Iris* No. 33, 10 in., 8 in., 6 in. $10.00, $6.50, $4.50 ea.

*Name created by the authors.

VASE	ROSE BOWL
Lady's Slipper* No. 6, 11 in. $10.00 ea.	Rose No. 63 $7.50 ea.

VASE			OIL CRUET
Rose 2 in. dia.	Daffodil*	Rose 2 in. dia.	Daisy (conventional) $5.00 ea.

*Name created by the authors.

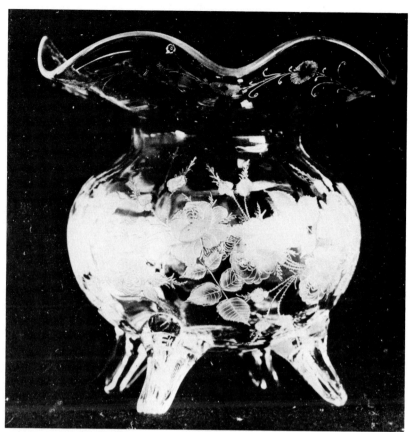

Bibliography

ENGLISH AND CAMEO GLASS

Beard, Geoffrey W., *Nineteenth-Century Cameo Glass* (Newport, Monmouthshire, England: Ceramic Book Company, 1956).

The Corning Museum of Glass, *English Nineteenth-Century Cameo Glass* (Corning, New York: The Corning Museum of Glass, 1963).

Goldstein, Sidney M., Leonard S. Rakow, and Juliette K. Rakow, *Cameo Glass: Masterpieces from 2000 Years of Glassmaking* (Corning, New York: The Corning Museum of Glass, 1982).

Revi, Albert C., *Nineteenth-Century Glass* (New York: Thomas Nelson and Sons, 1967).

ART GLASS AND LIBBEY PERIOD

Amberina, 1884 & 1917 (Toledo, Ohio: Antique & Historic Glass Foundation). A reprint of an 1884 Joseph Locke sketchbook with New England Glasswork's price list.

Fauster, Carl U., *Libbey Glass Since 1818* (Toledo, Ohio: Len Beach Press, 1979).

Ferson, Regis F., and Mary Fleming Ferson, *Yesterday's Milk Glass Today* (Pittsburgh, Pennsylvania: Regis and Mary Ferson, Publishers, 1981).

Grover, Ray, and Lee Grover, *Art Glass Nouveau* (Rutland, Vermont: Charles E. Tuttle Company, 1967).

Libbey Glass: A Tradition of 150 Years (Toledo, Ohio: The Toledo Museum of Art, 1968).

Revi, Albert C., "Joseph Locke's Amberina Sketchbook," *Hobbies*, vol. 61, no. 2, April 1956.

LOCKE ART GLASSWARE AND TECHNOLOGY

"Annual Meeting of Glass Men," *The Crockery and Glass Journal*, July 20, 1905, pp. 24–26.

Baer, Nell Jaffe, "Joseph Locke and His Art Glass," *Auction* (Parke Bernet Galleries), vol. 11, no. 8, reproduction p. 1, April 1969, p. 9.

Daniel, Dorothy, *Cut and Engraved Glass: 1771–1905* (New York: M. Barrows and Company, Inc., 1971).

Dreppard, Carl W., *A.B.C.'s of Old Glass* (Garden City, New York: Doubleday and Company, Inc., 1949).

Harris, Joel Chandler, *Tales from Uncle Remus* (New York, New York: Black Heritage Library Collection, Arno Press, Inc.).

Higgins & Seiter, Inc., *Rich Cut Glass and Fine China* (New York, ca. 1905).

Hodkin, F. W., and A. Cousin, *A Textbook of Glass Technology* (New York: D. Van Nostrand Company, 1925).

John Wanamaker, *Catalog of Crockery and China* (Philadelphia, ca. 1880).

Krak, J. B., "The Laboratory," *The Glass Industry*, vol. 2, 1921.

Locke, Joseph H., and Jane T. Locke, "Locke Art Glassware: Its Functional Shapes and Etched Designs," *Hobbies*, January 1985, vol. 89, no. 11.

Pincus, A. G., *Secondary Manufacturing in the Glass Industry* (New York: Books for Industry and The Glass Industry, Magazines for Industry, Inc., 1978)

Rood, Martha L., "One of Pittsburgh's Real Artists," *The Index* (Pittsburgh), July 8, 1916.

Silverman, Alexander, "Joseph Locke, Artist," *The Glass Industry*, vol. 17, no. 8, 1936.

Winterthur Museum Analytical Laboratory, Wilmington, Delaware; "Report No. 1593, 7/27/84," by Janice H. Carlson.

Index

acid work, 9, 10, 13
Agata, 5, 7, 8
Almond, Indian, 36, 37
Amberina, 5, 7
Art Glass Nouveau, 7

Baseball Catcher, 32, 33
Baseball Thrower, 34, 35
Beard, Geoffrey, 6
Berry, 10, 34, 35, 42, 43, 44, 45, 58, 59
    Monogram, 42, 43
Berry & Strawberry, 38, 39
bon-bon, 9, 38, 39
    footed, 13, 36, 38
Boston and Sandwich Glass Company, 6
Brer Rabbit, 11, 18, 19
Butterfly & Wheat, 34, 35, 56, 57

Cambridge Works (New England Glass
    Company), 7
Canoeist, 32, 33
Carder, Frederick, 6
champagne, 15, 28, 29
    saucer, 28, 29, 30, 31
    tall, 22, 23, 28, 29, 30, 31
Cherry, 10, 11
Chicken & Egg, 20, 21, 26, 27
claret, 28, 29, 30, 31
Clematis, 26, 27, 34, 35
cocktail, 28, 29, 30, 31, 44, 45
comport, 9, 14, 40, 41
    footed, 40, 41
"conventional," 11, 12
cordial, 28, 29, 42, 43, 44, 45
    tall, 28, 29, 42, 43
crème de menthe, 28, 29, 30, 31, 44, 45
Cresent, 30, 31
cruet, oil, 60, 61
Cupid, 58, 59
Currant, 10, 11, 36, 37
Cyclamen, 24, 25, 34, 35

Daffodil, 60, 61
Daisy, 10, 20, 21, 22, 23, 60, 61
decanter, 9, 13, 15, 42, 43, 44, 45
Deer, Antlered, 32, 33
Dog, Hunting, 34, 35
Dorflinger, C., and Sons, 15
du Pont, Henry Francis, Winterthur
    Museum, 14

Ebberts, E. P., 15
egg, 20, 21, 26, 27, 28, 29
Egyptian, 10, 11, 48, 49
Elks, B.P.O.E., 34, 35
Encore, 11
etched design, 10–12

Fauster, Carl U., 7
Fern, 20, 21
Ferson, Regis and Mary, 8
Fine Arts Department, University of
    Pittsburgh, 10
fingerbowl, 9, 28, 29, 30, 31, 34, 35
Fish, 18, 19, 20, 21, 26, 27, 34, 35
Fisherman, 34, 35
Forget-Me-Not, 10, 20, 21, 22, 23, 24, 25,
    28, 29, 30, 31, 34, 35, 46, 47, 48, 49
Fuchsia, 16, 17, 18, 19, 32, 33

Gillander and Sons, 15
glass blanks, 13, 14
Gleason, M. W., 15
goblet, 12, 14, 15, 22, 23, 28, 29, 30, 31,
    46, 47, 48, 49
    cut-stem, 22, 23, 24, 25
    short-stem, 24, 25
Goldstein, Sidney M., 6
Golfer, 34, 35
Good Shepherd, 11
Gooseberry, 36, 37
Grape, 10, 11, 22, 23, 24, 25, 26, 27, 32,
    33, 34, 35, 36, 37, 38, 39, 46, 47, 52,
    53
Grape & Lines, 10, 16, 17, 18, 19, 20, 21,
    22, 23, 24, 25, 30, 31, 40, 41, 46, 47,
    48, 49, 52, 53, 54, 55, 56, 57
    Monogram, 52, 53
grapefruit, 14, 38, 39
Grecian, 20, 21, 40, 41
    (anthemion), 20, 21
"grind, first," 8, 13
"grind, second," 8
Grover, Ray and Lee, 7
Guest Brothers, 6

Harris, Joel Chandler, 10
Heisey, A. H., 15
Henry Francis du Pont Winterthur
    Museum, 14
Hiawatha, 46, 47

Higgens & Seiter, 15
Hodgetts, William, 6
Hodgetts and Richardson, 6
Horse & Rider, 32, 33, 46, 47
Hunter & Dog, 32, 33
Hunt Institute for Botanical Docu-
    mentation, Carnegie-Mellon
    University, 10

ice, saucer-footed, 20, 21, 28, 29
Iris, 12, 56, 57, 58, 59
Ivy, 10, 18, 19, 20, 21, 26, 27, 48, 49

jug, 9
Juniper Berry, 18, 19

Lace & Lines, 34, 35
Lady's Slipper, 54, 55, 56, 57, 60, 61
Lechevrel, Alphonse-Eugène, 6
Lemon, 13, 18, 19
Libbey, Edward Drummond, 5, 7
Libbey, William L., 7
Libbey, W. L., and Sons, Company, 8
Libbey Glass, 6, 7, 13, 15
Libbey Glass Company, 7
Libbey Glass Since 1818, 7
Locke, Edward (father of Joseph), 5
Locke, Edward (half brother of Joseph), 5
Locke, Frank, 11
Locke, Joseph, 5–15
Locke, Joseph Edward (Ted), 6
Locke, May, 11
Locke, T. Hubert (Bert), 11
Locke Art Glassware, 5, 8, 9, 10, 11, 12, 13,
    14, 15
Locke Art Glassware Company, 5, 9
loving cup, 44, 45

Maize, 5, 7, 8
Morning Glory, 38, 39, 54, 55
motifs, 9, 10–11

nappie, 9, 38, 39
Nasturtium, 12
New England Glass Company, 6, 7, 8
Nineteenth-Century Glass, 7
Northwood, John, I, 6
Nut, 10

Oak Leaf & Acorn, 24, 25, 32, 33

"optic," 14
Orange, 13
Oyster, 20, 21, 24, 25, 26, 27
oyster cocktail, 20, 21, 26, 27, 28, 29

parfait, 26, 27
Pargeter and Company, 6
Paris Exposition (1878), 6
patents, 7, 8
Patti, Adelina, 11
Peachblow, 5, 7
Phoenix Glass, 15
Pineapple, 11
Pineapple & Grape, 10, 40, 41
pitcher, 12, 14, 46, 47, 48, 49, 50, 51
Plated Amberina, 7
Poinsettia, 12
Polo, 22, 23
Pomona, 5, 7, 13
Poppy, 10, 12, 36, 37, 52, 53
port, 28, 29, 30, 31
Portland Vase, 6
price, 14, 15
Primrose, 54, 55

Rakow, Dr. and Mrs. Leonard S., 6
Raspberry, 11
Rebecca at the Well, 11
Revi, Albert Christian, 6, 7
Rood, Martha L., 6
Rooster & Cherries, 30, 31

Rose, 10, 12, 16, 17, 20, 21, 22, 23, 24, 25,
    32, 33, 34, 35, 36, 37, 38, 39, 40, 41,
    44, 45, 48, 49, 54, 55, 58, 59, 60, 61
Rose & Lines, 50, 51
rose bowl, 60, 61
Royal Worcester China Factory, 5
Royal Worcester Company, 5, 6

Sailboat, 34, 35
Shamrock, 28, 29, 42, 43, 44, 45
sherbet, 28, 29
    saucer-footed, 13, 14, 20, 21, 28, 29
    stem, 30, 31
sherrie, 28, 29, 30, 31, 42, 43
signature, Locke Art, 9, 11, 12
Silverman, Alexander, 11, 13
stein, 9, 32, 33, 34, 35
stemware, 9, 13
Strawberry, 10, 11, 12, 38, 39
sugar and creamer, 14, 52, 53
Sweethearts, 50, 51

tankard, 48, 49
templates, 12
Tennis Woman, 34, 35
Thistle, 10, 16, 17, 18, 19, 24, 25
Thistle & Crown, 22, 23
Three Fruit, 20, 21
Tiffany & Co., 7
trademark, 9

tumbler, 9, 10, 14, 15, 16, 17, 18, 19, 24, 25,
    28, 29, 48, 49, 50, 51, 52, 53
    footed, 24, 25

Uncle Remus, 10
United States Glass Company, 5, 8, 9

vase, 9, 40, 41, 54, 55, 56, 57, 58, 59, 60,
    61
    sweet pea, 54, 55
    two-handled, 56, 57, 58, 59
Violet, 10, 28, 29, 32, 33
Violet & Lines, 16, 17

Wagner operas, 11
Wanamaker, John, 15
water bottle, 52, 53
Water Lily, 34, 35, 52, 53
Webb, Thomas, and Corbett, 6
Wheat, 18, 19
whiskey, 18, 19, 42, 43
Wild Rose, 5, 7, 8, 44, 45
Wild Rose & Lines, 50, 51
wine, 28, 29
    Moselle, 28, 29
    Rhine, 28, 29
    white, 30, 31
Winterthur Museum, 14
Woman at Churn, 32, 33
Woman Golfer, 34, 35, 50, 51
Woman with Flute, 50, 51
Woodall, George, 6